As a former constitutional lawyer who later taught classes at  the University of Chicago, Barack Obama should be a vigilant protector of the integrity of our electoral system. Indeed, as a U.S. senator from Illinois, he introduced a bill in 2007 to increase the criminal penalty for voter intimidation. "Both parties at different periods in our history have been guilty in different regions of preventing people from voting for a tactical advantage," he said at the time. "We should be beyond that."

He was right to be concerned. A Rasmussen Reports survey in 2008 found that 17 percent of Americans believe that large numbers of legitimate voters are prevented from voting. A slightly larger number, 23 percent, believe that large numbers of ineligible people are allowed to vote. That means two out of five Americans effectively believe our elections aren't free and fair.

Such cynicism is borne out by the widespread evidence that has accumulated over the past few years proving that the basic fairness of our elections is under assault from all sides:

- The radical organization ACORN (Association of Community Organizations for Reform Now) and other voter-registration groups have been frequently caught putting fraudulent names on voter rolls.

- A growing number of residents in states such as New York and New Jersey have homes in Florida and other states with milder climates and wind up registering and voting in both places.

- Legitimate and longtime voters sometimes find their names removed from registration lists by inaccurate purging.

- "Mickey Mouse," "Mary Poppins" and "Dick Tracy" are just some of the names showing up on registration lists along with many real individuals who are not eligible to vote.

- Arbitrary decision-making is on the increase in very close elections, as the Florida

2000 presidential recount and the 2008 Senate race in Minnesota demonstrate. There is growing uncertainty as to who is entitled to cast ballots and whose ballots should be counted.

These and other problems cry out for repair. But now that he is in the White House, President Obama, far from using his new powers to restore Americans' faith in their elections, has moved in exactly the opposite direction. The full story of how this presidency has further undermined our election processes provides a disturbing look into one of the most significant threats our democracy faces today.

Justice Lets the New Black Panthers Walk

Bartle Bull couldn't believe his eyes. The former civil-rights lawyer had been arrested in the South during the 1960s. He once forced local officials in Mississippi to remove nooses that were hanging from tree branches outside polling places. But until election day 2008 in Philadelphia, he had never seen a man brandishing a weapon blocking the entrance to a polling place. And now, he can't understand why the Obama Department of Justice has dropped its case against the New Black Panther Party, the hate group (according to the Southern Poverty Law Center and the Anti-Defamation League) whose thugs he saw threatening potential voters with truncheons when they tried to vote.

Bull, who was once Robert Kennedy's New York presidential campaign manager and is a former publisher of the left-wing *Village Voice*, has moderated his politics, going as far as to join Democrats for McCain in 2008. It was in that capacity that he traveled to Philadelphia on election day. When he visited a polling place at 12th and Fairmount, he found two men dressed in black combat boots, black berets and black uniforms, blocking the door. One was brandishing a large police-style nightstick.

McCain volunteers called the police, and

media filmed the whole incident. The police ordered the armed man to leave but did not take away his weapon. But one of his colleagues didn't go quietly. Minister King Samir Shabazz, head of the New Black Panther Party in Philadelphia, yelled at onlookers, "You are about to be ruled by the black man, cracker!"

In March 2009, Bull got a call from Christian Adams, an attorney with the Justice Department's Civil Rights Division, who asked him to provide an affidavit about the incident to support a civil-rights lawsuit against the New Black Panther Party and three of its supporters, one of whom, Jerry Jackson, is an elected member of Philadelphia's 14th Ward Democratic Committee and, as recently as spring 2009, has served as an official poll watcher in a local election. Bull said he would, provided that the Justice Department follow through on the lawsuit to the very end.

The lawsuit was filed, and when none of the defendants answered it, a federal court in Philadelphia rendered a default judgment against the defendants. Bull was astonished, therefore, when the government reacted by suddenly dropping charges against the New Black Panther Party and the two defendants. Another defendant was given only the mild sanction of being barred from displaying a weapon near a polling place for the next three years.

A Justice Department spokesman issued a terse statement saying only that the department made its decision "based on a careful assessment of the facts and the law." Career Justice Department attorneys told Bull that they were appalled by this inexplicable failure to enforce the Voting Rights Act. Those near the case believe that the decision was politically motivated – a signal sent, according to Bull, that "intimidation against poll watchers challenging the fraudulent voters registered by ACORN" may be permissible.

Hans von Spakovsky, a former official in the Justice Department's Civil Rights Division under President George W. Bush, told me he was shocked by the department's turnaround in the Philadelphia case: "Imagine if the defendants had been white and been intimidating voters and Justice had dropped the case. There would have been a political earthquake." In the wake of the Justice Department's action, the U.S. Commission on Civil Rights voted on Aug. 7, 2009, to send a letter to the department expanding its own investigation and demanding more complete answers. "We believe the Department's defense of its actions thus far undermines respect for rule of law," its letter stated.

Bull plans to keep the issue alive. "When he took office, Attorney General Eric Holder stated that America was a nation of 'cowards' when it comes to race and that he was going to make civil-rights cases a top priority," he told me. "But who are today's 'cowards' on race? This kind of double standard is not what Martin Luther King and Robert Kennedy fought for."

* * *

Playing With the Numbers:
The 2010 Census

The national census – supposedly an objective counting of every inhabitant of a country – has always taken place with politics lurking in the background. Jesus was born in Bethlehem because the Romans insisted Joseph and Mary go back to the town of their birth to be counted for tax purposes. The 1937 Soviet census was annulled because it showed a sharp drop in population resulting from the famines and killings of the Stalin era; a "correct" census was held in 1939 after the administrators of the first one had been shipped to the gulag.

Now, Obama is making the upcoming 2010 census a case of politics by other means. In February 2009, GOP Sen. Judd Gregg withdrew his nomination to head the Department of Commerce partly in response to the administration's decision that the director of the Census Bureau would no longer report to the commerce secretary, but to the White

House. Gregg was upset at the prospect of political operatives using computer models and "sampling" techniques to adjust the census count upward on "underrepresented" groups. *The Philadelphia Inquirer* called the proposed move "a threat to the fairness and accuracy of the census."

Liberal groups have long believed that up to 8 million members of minority groups and the homeless were not picked up in the 2000 census. To make up for these supposedly "missing people," sampling-based adjustments would be used to add people to the actual count all the way down to the neighborhood and block levels. Those "adjusted" numbers would have real political significance because they would redraw congressional and state legislative districts to allocate federal money.

In 1999, the Supreme Court ruled 5 to 4 that sampling could not be used to reapportion congressional seats among the states. But the court left open the possibility that sampling could be used to redraw political boundaries within the states. My sources inside the

Census Bureau tell me that, assurances from Obama appointees to the contrary, sampling is about to make a comeback.

The problem with sampling-adjusted numbers is that they don't add up. In theory, statisticians may be able to generally identify the number of people missed in a head count, but they cannot then place those abstract "missing people" into specific neighborhoods, let alone blocks. Starting in 2000, the Census Bureau conducted three years of studies with the help of many outside statistical experts and concluded that "adjustment based on sampling" could damage census credibility. Rather than "enfranchising" minority groups, as its proponents piously claim, such a procedure exaggerates their numbers. "The adjusted numbers told us the head count had over-counted the number of Indians on reservations," former Census Director Louis Kincannon says. "That made no sense."

Robert Gibbs, Obama administration press secretary, insists that "historical precedent" exists for the White House to ride close herd on the census, but every living former census director supports a pending bill in Congress to make the Census Bureau an independent agency and further insulate it from politics. Even the liberal *San Francisco Chronicle* was appalled at the White House power play: "Allowing Obama politicos like chief of staff Rahm Emanuel – a top House Democratic strategist in his prior life – anywhere near the census adding machine is ... a Chicago-style setup that should worry any voter."

When President Obama met with Sen. Gregg at the White House the day before Gregg's withdrawal, Obama could have simply told him he hadn't known of the White House power grab and claimed that the Census Bureau would continue to report directly to the commerce secretary. But he didn't, and that refusal played a major role in Gregg's decision to withdraw. It was clear to him that in having to decide between his vaunted new "politics of transparency" and the left-wing pressure groups, Obama had chosen to side with the liberal base of his party.

In having to decide between his vaunted new "politics of transparency" and the left-wing pressure groups, Obama had chosen to side with the liberal base of his party.

The result of this maneuvering, according to the Government Accountability Office, will be "serious trouble" for the 2010 census. The Census Bureau form will not ask if people are citizens. Its goal is to count all people physically present in the country, including large numbers who are here illegally. By counting the somewhere between 7 million and 12 million illegal aliens now in the U.S., some states will gain a big advantage when it comes to the reapportionment of congressional seats. One likely potential winner under the new White House rules will be California, which stands to gain nine more seats in Congress than it would if only U.S. citizens were counted. States like Ohio, Louisiana, Michigan and Pennsylvania could be among the losers.

The net result? The census will become a political football, especially over the issue of sampling, which many experts say is too primitive a tool to be trusted with something as important as the census. And our citizens will feel correctly that their votes have been devalued by the extent of the White House's involvement in the process.

Universal Voter Confusion

When Congress passed the Help America Vote Act, or HAVA, in 2002, its lead Democratic sponsor, Sen. Chris Dodd of Connecticut, praised it for "making it easier to vote and harder to steal."

HAVA's most important reforms required that states meet two "minimum standards" in conducting their elections. The first is setting up a centralized, statewide voter registration list to avoid duplications, and limiting how often a flawed voter list prevents someone from voting. The second is a requirement that every voter in every state be allowed to cast a "provisional" ballot if he or she shows up at a precinct and finds that his or her name is not on the registration list. If the authorities determine after the polls close that the voter was eligible, the vote counts. If the ballot is ruled invalid, the voter can discover that fact and ascertain the reasons why at a toll-free telephone number or Web site.

HAVA was a genuinely bipartisan piece of legislation, winning support from the then-Democratic Senate and the GOP-controlled House. But it didn't approach, let alone solve, the problem of our corrupted voter registration rolls. Curtis Gans, director of the Center for the Study of the American Electorate, estimates that "there are at least 20 million names on the registration lists who should not be there, who have died, or moved or who are not legitimate voters." And the set of legislative proposals the Obama administration has prepared for passage in this session of Congress – chief among them, "universal voter registration" – will only make those lists less accurate. In mandating a federal takeover of voter registration from the states that would greatly increase the chances of fraud, in fact, they would reduce public confidence in our elections, create logistical nightmares for election officials and enhance the opportunity to commit fraud.

The idea, embraced by Barack Obama when he was a presidential candidate, is to shift responsibility for registering to vote from the individual to the federal government. All eligible citizens would automatically be registered to vote, with existing lists such as DMV records, income-tax returns, welfare rolls and unemployment lists being used to enroll everyone. Once registered, individuals would stay on the federal rolls, even if they move to another state or district.

The new rules are based on the claim of liberal groups that a major reason for the low turnout in American elections is the difficulty of registering to vote. But the evidence belies this. We just held a presidential election that produced the third-highest turnout in our nation's history since women were granted the right to vote in 1920. The Census Bureau reports there was an increase of 4 million registered voters in 2008, and turnout was up by 5 million voters. Yet 13 states recorded lower turnout, including five of the eight states that have same-day election registration. "It is incandescently clear that the primary determinant of turnout is no longer procedure but motivation," says a study from the Center for the Study of the American Electorate.

The databases that proponents of the bill plan to draw on – such as driver's licenses and social services and tax records – lack critical information about voter eligibility, such as citizenship status. They also contain the names of people who are certified to be mentally incompetent or are felons, making them ineligible to vote under most state laws. Because an increasing number of people own property in more than one place or pay taxes to more than one government entity, universal voter registration would automatically register them in more than one location, allowing them to vote more than once – either in person or by mail.

Von Spakovsky, a former member of the Federal Election Commission now with the Heritage Foundation, says that universal voter registration "would automate voter registration fraud and decrease the security and integrity of our election process to deal with a nonexistent problem."

The idea of universal voter registration was inspired by laws in several states that allow election day registration, permitting people to both register and vote at the polls at the same time. But the states that have tried same-day registration are mostly small, with stable populations and long traditions of good government. Even so, there have been problems. In 1986, for instance, Oregon voters overwhelmingly scrapped the idea after a cult that wanted to take over a town government tried to register hundreds of supporters on election day. In 2000, a New York socialite working for Al Gore scandalized Wisconsin when a TV camera caught her bribing street vagrants with packs of cigarettes if they registered and voted that day.

Even liberal states such as California and Colorado recently voted down same-day registration. The more that average people learn about the idea, the more they turn against it. It would be nice to think that the U.S. Congress can withstand pressure from the White House as it goes through a similar learning process.

Ironically, the recent scandals that have engulfed the voter registration group ACORN could provide a perverse argument by liberals that universal voter registration is desirable. At an August 2009 meeting of Netroots Nation, the liberal blogging community, several activists said that ACORN's registration scandals point up the need to replace the current "chaotic" system of signing up voters with a "streamlined," nationally mandated system that signs up everybody.

Left unaddressed by such an argument is how stuffing voter rolls with millions of new registrants that have expressed no interest in voting won't create an automatic pool of names that vote fraudsters could mine to cast illegal ballots – either through absentee programs or in-person voting at polling places.

Nullifying the Law

The Justice Department's charge – applying the law in an objective manner without political consideration – often involves a delicate balancing act, since political appointees set the department's policies and priorities. But the Obama Justice Department appears not even to have tried for balance and fairness in the brief time Obama has been in office. Instead, as its approach to voter registration shows, it has clearly and consistently chosen to misinterpret and misapply election laws for what appear to be political motives.

The federal 2002 HAVA requires states to coordinate their voter registration lists with other databases, such as Social Security records and driver's license lists, and to "verify the accuracy of the information provided on applications for voter registration."

Georgia, for instance, moved to comply with this federal requirement by passing a law in 2008 setting up a verification procedure that included checking to see if the potential voter was a citizen. (It is against both federal and state law for noncitizens to register or vote.) Georgia consulted with career Justice Department employees in 2008 in writing its rules.

Its program worked well. Using existing databases, Georgia flagged 4,000 potential noncitizens and sent them letters asking them

The Obama Justice Department appears not even to have tried for balance and fairness in the brief time Obama has been in office.

to verify their citizenship status. More than 2,000 failed to comply, making it likely many were indeed not eligible to vote.

Minority turnout in Georgia was hardly affected by the new rules. In fact, between 2004 and 2008, Hispanic turnout increased by 140 percent, and black turnout increased by 42 percent. But on May 29, 2009, the Obama Justice Department used its power under the Voting Rights Act to veto Georgia's verification law. It claimed it would have a "disparate impact" on minority voters. The evidence? It cited findings that Asians and Hispanics were supposedly "twice as likely to appear on the list" of potential noncitizens as whites.

Of course, there is a ready explanation for this. Only 35 percent of Hispanics and 58 percent of Asians in Georgia are citizens. Although no evidence has been presented that anyone was prevented from voting in 2008 because they were improperly listed as noncitizens, the Justice Department's veto of Georgia's law held.

The Justice Department's about-face on

citizenship requirements isn't the only case in which it has demonstrated a troubling double standard. Missouri, to use another example, has a long record of conflict with the federal government on the issue of bad registration records. At the time of the 2008 election, for instance, more than a dozen Missouri counties had more registered voters than the number of adults over the age of 18. Under the Bush administration, the attorney general had gone before the Eighth Circuit Court of Appeals and won a ruling to force the Missouri secretary of state's office to clean up its registration lists. But in March 2009, the Obama Justice Department dismissed this lawsuit – its own lawsuit – without explanation. As in the case of the New Black Panther Party voter intimidation case it would abandon two months later, the Justice Department had effectively already won but nonetheless decided to surrender its victory. What kind of prosecutors act that way? The answer appears to be: highly political ones.

"The Justice Department is charged with

securing the integrity of the voter registration process," notes von Spakovsky. "In just the first year of its time in office, this administration appears to be moving as fast as it can to evade those responsibilities."

From Little Oaks Grows a Mighty Acorn

Democrats are split on how to deal with ACORN, the liberal "community organizing" group that deployed thousands of get-out-the-vote workers for Barack Obama in the last election. State and city Democratic officials – who've been contending with its many scandals – are moving against the organization. But in Washington, Democrats are still sweeping ACORN abuses under a rug.

In July, the minority members of the House Committee on Oversight and Government Reform issued a report claiming that ACORN "is a shell game played in 120 cities, 43 states and the District of Columbia through a complex structure designed to conceal illegal activities, to use taxpayer and tax-exempt dollars for partisan political purposes, and to distract investigators."

After examining ACORN's interlocked networks of command and control, the report claimed that the group deliberately organized

---

In Washington, Democrats are still sweeping ACORN abuses under a rug.

---

itself in such a way as to escape legal and public scrutiny: "ACORN hides behind a paper wall of nonprofit corporate protections to conceal a criminal conspiracy on the part of its directors, to launder federal money in order to pursue a partisan political agenda and to manipulate the American electorate."

In May 2009, Nevada officials charged ACORN, its regional director and its Las Vegas field director with submitting thousands of fraudulent voter registration forms.

Larry Lomax, registrar of voters in Las Vegas, says he believes 48 percent of ACORN's forms "are clearly fraudulent." That same month, prosecutors in Pittsburgh also charged seven ACORN employees with filing hundreds of fraudulent voter registrations before the 2008 general election.

ACORN spokesman Scott Levenson calls the Nevada criminal complaint "political grandstanding" and says that any problems were the actions of an unnamed "bad employee." But Catherine Cortez Masto, Nevada's Democratic attorney general, told the *Las Vegas Sun* that ACORN itself is named in the criminal complaint. She says that ACORN's training manuals "clearly detail, condone and ... require illegal acts."

The upcoming trial of the Las Vegas ACORN officials could see further revelations. Christopher Edwards, former ACORN Las Vegas field director, has agreed to plead to two counts of conspiracy to commit the crime of compensation for registration of voters and will testify against former ACORN

Regional Director Amy Busefink and ACORN itself, which is a co-defendant in the case.

Meanwhile, other cities have beefs with ACORN. Fred Voight, deputy election commissioner in Philadelphia, protested after ACORN submitted at least 1,500 fraudulent registrations in fall 2008. "This has been going on for a number of years," he told CNN in October. Democrat Matthew Potter, St. Louis's deputy elections director, had similar complaints. In the 2008 election, ACORN's practices led to investigations, some ongoing, in 14 other states.

The stink is bad enough that some congressional Democrats took notice. At a March 19, 2009, hearing on election problems, Michigan Rep. John Conyers Jr., chairman of the House Judiciary Committee, pressed New York Rep. Jerrold Nadler, chairman of the Subcommittee on the Constitution, Civil Rights and Civil Liberties, to hold a hearing on ACORN. Nadler agreed to consider the request.

But then Conyers changed his mind, releasing a statement through his office saying that after reviewing "the complaints against ACORN, I have concluded that a hearing on this matter appears unwarranted at this time." A Democratic staffer told me he believes the House leadership put pressure on Conyers to back down.

Barney Frank, the chairman of the House Financial Services Committee, followed the same pattern. In April, he voted for a committee amendment to the Mortgage Reform and Anti-Predatory Lending Act by Rep. Michelle Bachmann (R-Minn.) to block groups indicted on voter fraud from receiving federal housing or legal assistance grants. Identical language was passed into law in the Housing and Economic Recovery Act of 2008. Frank then reversed course and said he "had not read [the amendment] carefully" before backing it. He gutted the amendment on the House floor in May 2009, claiming that the language Congress passed just last year is "a violation of the basic principles of due process."

Money – a lot of it – is at stake, in addition

to foot soldiers pounding the pavement for Democrats in national and local elections. In the stimulus bill passed by Congress, ACORN is eligible, along with other activist groups, to apply for $2 billion in funds to redevelop abandoned and foreclosed homes.

Anita MonCrief, an ACORN whistle-blower, says the problems run deep. Mon-Crief worked at Project Vote, an ACORN affiliate, in late 2007. She says its development director, Karen Gillette, told her she had direct contact with the Obama campaign and also told her to call Obama donors who had maxed out on donations to the candidate but who could contribute to ACORN. Project Vote calls her charges "absolutely false." (Gillette has declined comment.)

ACORN's relationship with the Obama campaign is a matter of public record. Last year, Citizens Consulting Inc., the umbrella group controlling ACORN, was paid $832,000 by the Obama campaign for get-out-the-vote efforts in key primary states. In filings with the Federal Election Commission, the campaign listed the payments as "staging, sound, lighting," only correcting them after reporters from the *Pittsburgh Tribune-Review* revealed their true nature.

Obama distanced himself from the group's scandals in 2008, saying, "We don't need ACORN's help." Nevertheless, he got his start as a community organizer at ACORN's side. In 1992, he headed a registration effort for Project Vote. In 1995, he represented ACORN in a key case upholding the new Motor Voter Act – the very law whose mandated postcard registration system ACORN workers use to flood election offices with bogus registrations.

But ACORN's registration tricks may soon be unnecessary. As mentioned earlier, congressional Democrats are backing a bill to mandate a nationwide database to automatically register driver's license holders or recipients of government benefits.

This "would create an engraved invitation for voter fraud," says former Minnesota Secretary of State Mary Kiffmeyer, who points out that these lists are filled with felons and noncitizens who are ineligible to vote. Ironically, in light of its troubles with the law, ACORN was selected in March to assist the U.S. census in reaching out to minority communities and recruiting census enumerators for the count next year.

For They Are Jolly Good Felons

Felony disenfranchisement laws keep an estimated 5.3 million Americans with felony convictions from the polls, including 2.1 million who no longer are in prison. Here, the Obama administration has shown admirable restraint in not proposing its own federal legislation on the issue. But it has also steadfastly refused to take a position on bills pending in Congress that would do just that, and leading civil-rights advocates say they are convinced the Obama administration would quietly sign such a bill.

At present, standards regarding felons' access to the ballot box vary greatly. Maine and Vermont let jailbirds vote from their prison cells. A total of 34 states and the District of Columbia automatically allow felons who've served their time in prison to vote. Eleven states restrict the right of felons to vote after their sentences are served, while 35 states prevent parolees from voting. A total of

---

It's easy to understand why "felon enfranchisement" is a liberal issue.

---

30 states ban those on probation from casting ballots. Legislation likely to be introduced would "rationalize" these disparate laws.

It's easy to understand why "felon enfranchisement" is a liberal issue. In a 2003 study, sociologists Christopher Uggen and Jeff Manza found that roughly a third of disenfranchised felons had completed their prison time or parole and would thus have their vote restored under such a bill. While only a bit more than a third of felons are African American, an overwhelming majority do lean toward one political party – Democrat. In presidential races, the two scholars estimated that Bill Clinton won 86 percent of the felon vote in 1992 and a whopping 93 percent four years later. Voting participation by all felons, Uggen and Manza estimated, would have allowed Democrats to win a series of key U.S. Senate elections, thus giving the party control of the Senate continuously from 1986 to 2004.

There is some evidence that felons already swing elections even in states where many of them are barred from voting. The *Seattle Times* found that 129 felons in just two counties, King and Pierce, voted illegally in the photo-finish race for governor in Washington in 2004, which Democrat Christine Gregoire won, coincidentally, by 129 votes.

The issue of felon voting might be a little broken, but a federal law won't fix it. We should leave the matter where the Constitution intended it be lodged – with the states. "If you're not willing to follow the law, then you can't claim a right to make the law for everyone else. And of course that's what [felons] are doing when [they] vote," says Roger Clegg of the conservative Center for Equal Opportunity. "Why should the federal government step in and determine a one-size-fits-all policy on felon voting?"

CONCLUSION

Americans are aware that our history includes painful examples of discriminatory hurdles to voting. They instinctively and justifiably resist anything that smacks of exclusion and oppose any attempt to create artificial barriers to voter participation. They also intuitively understand that when improperly cast ballots are counted or outright fraud countenanced, their civil rights are violated just as surely as if they were prevented from casting a ballot by a thug with a swagger stick.

Citizenship requires orderly, clear and vigorous procedures to ensure that the integrity of our elections – and voter confidence in them – is maintained. "The more clearly rules are settled in advance, the better elections we will have," says Brad King, a former state elections director of Minnesota. "What we don't want is the designed sloppiness that a few politicians allow to seep into our system through ambiguity and vagueness."

We also don't want the unequal application of the law, something that the Obama administration's early actions signal might be happening. Shying away from pursuing election cases even when the evidence is literally handed to prosecutors on videotape (the New Black Panther Party case) is troubling. By not enforcing laws mandating accurate and complete voter registration lists, the Obama administration is devaluing the most basic covenant between citizens and state. The impact on our system of self-governance is similar to what would happen to our economic system if the Treasury Department evinced no interest in containing the number of counterfeit bills circulating in the economy.

If we do not demand that the Obama administration and its allies in Congress abandon schemes and policies that further undermine confidence in our electoral system, we are headed for crises that will shake our electoral system and will make us look back on the disputed presidential vote of 2000 with something like nostalgia.

First American edition published in 2009 by Encounter Books,
an activity of Encounter for Culture and Education, Inc., a nonprofit,
tax exempt corporation. Encounter Books website address:
www.encounterbooks.com

Manufactured in the United States and printed on acid-free paper.
The paper used in this publication meets the minimum requirements
of ANSI/NISO z39.48–1992 (R 1997) (*Permanence of Paper*).

FIRST AMERICAN EDITION

LIBRARY OF CONGRESS CATALOGING-IN-PUBLICATION DATA

Fund, John H., 1957–
How the Obama administration threatens to undermine our elections
/ by John Fund.
p. cm. — (Encounter broadsides)
ISBN-13: 978-1-59403-461-9 (pbk. : alk. paper)
ISBN-10: 1-59403-461-3 (pbk. : alk. paper)
1. Elections—Corrupt practices—United States. 2. United States—
Politics and government—2009– 3. United States—Politics and
government—2001–2009. 4. Obama, Barack. I. Title.
JK1994.F85 2009
324.60973—dc22
2009036816

10 9 8 7 6 5 4 3 2 1